5555M ABOVE SEA LEVEL

where being lost is being found....

SRISHTI PAI

INDIA • SINGAPORE • MALAYSIA

ISBN

Hardcase 979-8-89724-526-0
Paperback 979-8-89699-488-6

About the Author

Srishti Pai is a 21 year old newly budding writer. Her love for backpacking, high altitude trekking, nature and adventure, is what drives her thought process to write creatively. Besides this, she is also a DJ, singer, photographer and a National level air rifle shooter. Currently working as a screenplay writer, she plans to do her masters in filmmaking and become an independent filmmaker and author. The theme of her writing revolves around 'making a space where it is okay to ruminate over one's thoughts and emotions', she also believes that in order to be in touch with yourself one has to be in touch with nature and adventure.

Authors Instagram – @srishti_pai

Authors business email – paisrisht@gmail.com

Disclaimer

All incidents, thoughts, pictures, and moments depicted in this book are solely based on personal experiences. They are not intended as references to any third party or as a means to demean anyone else's views. This book is created purely for recreational purposes and does not reflect any personal vendetta against any individual, place, or entity.

Table of Contents

Foreword

Sri,

Mountains. They're majestic, grand and absolutely humbling in every way.

After being on quite a few of them I've come to realise that they test character, patience, and values. They have done a number on me and one can never escape that feeling. It can shape a human being and it can break someone's ego.

And just like that this book explores those feelings and sentiments that one would feel when they face a 19000 ft tall mega structure whilst being a 5ft 6 inch human being.

It's funny how the human mind can feel such grand feelings at such grand heights while being so insignificant and tiny in front of it. It's a little bit like poetry that way, scaling a mountain and it's for you to now discover and immerse yourself in the lines of self expression, exploration and freedom. Peak into my sister's mind and look through not only her eyes but also her words in this collection of short poems and memories.

- Radhika Parikh

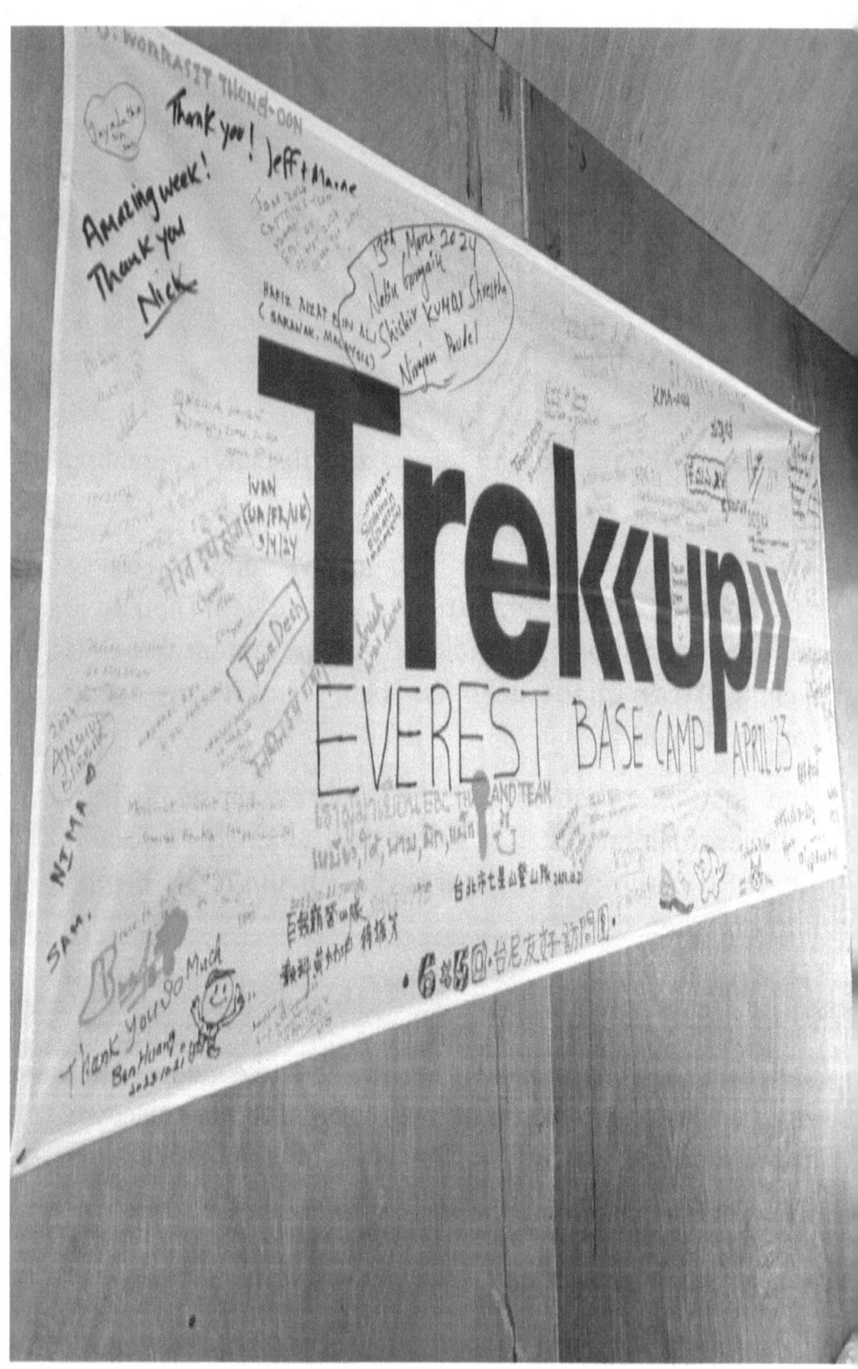

Coordinates – 27.7103° N, 85.3222° E

Preface

The thoughts and poetry that one will encounter were written in moments where I felt miles away from reality—literally. Each of these thoughts came to me while I was on a solo trek to the Everest Base Camp in Nepal, during the summer of 2024. I was there for twenty-two days. One relevant learning of each day is what I compiled into this book. Things I felt, sensed, and realized on that journey changed me internally. It was like a spiritual walk—heavenly, nothing like before. A journey where each day made me feel closer to the sky, truly enlightened, and gave me a sense of belonging. The content of this book consists of a few thoughts which played a pivotal role in transforming my life, and hopefully, it will transform yours too. Consider it like my personal diary that I let you read. They are not just poetic lines or thoughts but outcomes of the wildest and simplest of experiences that left me in a state of trance—a feeling similar to deep meditation. Those moments where everything around a person comes to a halt—where one feels different in their thought process. Written when I was daydreaming, yet a figment of my mind was very much in touch with that moment in which I realized them. Although my book is meant for daydreamers and lateral thinkers, men and women alike, the point of putting these thoughts out there is to put to sleep the ones wide awake. Pausing and daydreaming, when done the right way, is meditation for the subconscious. These pages are gateways to that portal where one can discover theirs. It's like a chain reaction I intend to create. When one feels overstimulated by the happenings around them, one paragraph from the aisle of my mind can be read like a lullaby—for falling asleep (mentally), rewiring a possible connection with an inner self, or awakening your inner child. They have a lot of questions they want answers for. I would suggest reading this from a child's perspective, whose minds are like blank slates. One might just be lucky if they succeed in this, because the experience that awaits them will be like a roller-coaster up to the clouds.

– The Author

DATE - 23-09-2024

...

Coordinates - 27.3938° N, 86.0601° E

Introduction

'5555m Above Sea Level' is not just a collection of poetic pieces... they are real thoughts which have an underlying introspective meaning to them. The moment one flips to the first page, they will start thinking from a very grey perspective. Nothing in this book is black or white. It is meant to touch those places of your mind and feelings which one wouldn't even think of. All these pieces have multiple layers to them, left to individual interpretation. These twenty-two pages, are enough to make one see moments, instances, and day-to-day conversations in general from a different perspective. One stops having a microscopic view of things. Consider this book as unlocking a third eye or a sixth sense—understanding moments from a spiritual point of view. Every page is like a learning experience for the day. Along with the collection of thoughts are pictures of the places where I got the very idea for these thoughts. To make it slightly more interesting, I have put down the coordinates of each place below the picture instead of the name of the place itself. Feel free to Google the coordinates when inquisitive about the exact location.:) The beauty of this book lies in the fact that when one reads the last page, it will automatically lead you back to the first one. The theme of this book is mindfulness. The content touches spheres like morals, values, empathy, ruthlessness, idleness, silence, nature, and existence in ways that one would not think of. Every piece touches a different topic, left for the reader to decipher in their own thoughtful language. Like a puzzle to solve, it leaves one intrigued. These thoughts are written in a way to be mulled over with a glass of red wine or with a cup of coffee or tea. They are not meant to be forcefully digressed or tried to make sense of. The understanding or interpretation of it should be natural and what you would like to make of it. In that way, it sticks with you throughout. These thoughts are for those especially who feel that they are different and who are made to feel being different is a bad thing. But if one wasn't different, how would he or she make a difference?

If you're lost, you're doing it right....

(In Memory of the Summer of '24)

Coordinates — 27.7400° N, 86.7126° E

The Backpacker's Ode

I would climb all mountains with you,
Just hold my hand.
Feel so blessed to meet you,
It wasn't planned.
The time I spent with you through those days,
Can never ever just be replaced.
I just wished we could spend some more time,
Every moment rewinds in my mind.
Sometimes we all meet by chance,
What remains, is the memories we form.

Coordinates – 27.8362° N, 86.7646° E

A Passerby's gift

There I stood, looking at the plain
blue slate above me,
Getting lost in its vastness,
I felt its calmness dawning upon me.
Its restfulness was so overbearing,
I could sense the chaos that
resided below its composed pretence,
And instantaneously I realized that
I had found an empathetic friend.

Coordinates — 27.6857° N, 86.7278° E

3

A Fool's Art

The heart, a frangible piece of art,
Ornamented with intricate mirrors,
reflecting truly cherished,
and deeply seated moments of the past.
Kept for display in a museum full of clowns,
It was left naked to the eyes of despise and denounce.
They laughed at the art which was indecipherable,
Little did they know that its beauty
was above and beyond a fool so despicable.

Coordinates — 27.6857° N, 86.7278° E

Queen of hearts

As I walked down the aisle of the
mystifying corners of my mind,
I couldn't help but pay heed,
to the shimmering ray of hope,
my brain tried to perceive.
It tried to emit light in every nook
and corner of my tainted shrine,
But alas! For my mind, succumbed to
the trickery of the devil in disguise.

Coordinates – 27.8069° N, 86.7140° E

The last laugh

He who seemingly quotes the vile absurd,
So aberrant a thought they look at him in awe.
Impenetrable his words into their superior matches,
For the thought so awful for a just belly to digest.
Wildly their laughs shadow his foresay,
The echoes made the fool cripple to his doomsday.

Coordinates — 27° 50'1" N, 86° 41'59.85" E

Behold

Just pause and commend the
miniscule details that encompass you,
The ones you discount and pass by
hastily without an overview.
By and by they crave your desperate
attention, for their sole purpose,
Is to feed your curiosity and introspection.
The longer your hiatus, the longer your breath,
The thoughts get clearer and the
moment is ceased with gratefulness.
For man was born as an admirer of life,
It's what makes himself effacing and truly alive.

Coordinates - 27.9595° N, 86.7899° E

Warmth of its safe haven

I sat one evening intoxicated by relentless thoughts,
Pensiveness... made me unaware of what was around.
Like a whirling tornado the cogitation wouldn't halt,
Its intensity consumed my every ounce.
I could feel myself seemingly wither to the ground,
In that moment, 'Tears 'was the
only armour I could mount.
Like a compassionate friend,
it understood my moroseness,
And sheltered me from the unforgiving distress.
Its warmth made my agony melt away,
No one had ever heard me the way it did that day.

Coordinates – 27.8069° N, 86.7140° E

The Philosophy of Being

As the nights and days pass,
I begin to realize that I am nothing
but a calamity kept at halt.
For, my death was ordained before I was born,
To exist in the present, with my thoughts
and actions is solely my purpose.
Cause neither yesterday was mine, nor tomorrow will.
I own and control nothing at all,
For I came as a visitor, and when I
finally hit the ground,
I will be remembered merely as a story
in the memory of my fellow visitors around.

Coordinates — 27.9312° N, 86.8047° E

A Just World's Reality

No more will a man be judged for
who he wants to be,
In my eyes, his beauty lies in
being truthful to his insight.
My soul dies to see the person he so wants to be,
Fortunately, this friendly world has some
stringent rules for it's survivors.
It took long for it to get seeped into my reality,
that honest souls are like unarmed
soldiers on a battlefield.

Coordinates - 27.8923° N, 86.8314° E

100m above Dingboche

I woke up one morning surrounded by mist,
The weather around me awoke my dooming spirit.
Enthralled by the optimism that contained me,
I was ready to take up the day thoughtlessly with glee.
There stood Tul "100m above Dingboche we will go"
Relentlessly my mind decided to go with the flow.
Across the table my teammates sat dejected and low,
Rising up I decided to reverse their pessimistic approach.
Invigoration is what their heart needed the most,
The sanguineness driving my motivation
struck a chord with their soul.
They all stood with their head held high,
Together we walked one step at a time,
There stood the red flag waving our way,
The walk I remember till date,
It was called '100m above Dingboche'.

Coordinates – 27.9343° N, 86.7819° E

The gatekeeper

When I look at my reflection on the
calm surfaces of your eyes,
In it I saw something deep, something
beyond what a delicate being could see.
How intensely it came crashing, the
multitude of waves waiting to touch the shore.
I stood there on gold sand, a force calling me to
explore what was beneath its light blue walls.
As I went towards the waves, they receded away, so
fast was my pace but the blue line
just went beyond my trace.
There awakened a sandstorm that blinded my sight,
And....no more could I see what
was left of those blue eyes.

Coordinates — 27.6857° N, 86.7278° E

Lucid blues

Why are you scared?
Is it in your mind?
I can see you there
Standing like its fine.
Well, is it okay?
If I sat beside you?
Would you feel okay
If I sat beside you?
Just show me your pain
You will be alright
It will be okay
If you close your eyes
And feel what's inside.

Coordinates – 27.9233° N, 86.8056° E

13

An honest act

For if the world was perceived unmasked,
The reality would look so different at large.
Through the transparency the truth would unfold,
No more would a man be deceived,
For his eyes would see the world for
what it was, rather than
What it ought to be...

Coordinates — 27.6857° N, 86.7278° E

Cheshire Cat's effect

Smile Smile a big wide smile,
Look at me...now you're happy.
No matter what goes down,
She said- always give a big wide smile.
Today, I followed the quote she said,
Stretched my muscles up till my earlobes,
She was sleeping still in front of me.
They all looked at me puzzled in their expression
A big wide smile I gave in return.

Coordinates – 27.9312° N, 86.8047° E

An Underdogs Tale

A path sauntered by many anew,
Chained up each to the other unswerving.
Running down gained them nothing new,
Determined their passage continues.
"Behold!" says one acquiescently they halt.
Yes sire, my sire, they nod their tops.
Days go by, their hopes hold them steady and high.
The sires laughed at their obedient cries
Poor lot, they would never realize.

Coordinates − 27.9233° N, 86.8056° E

In other words

Caring to me my broken love,
is in ways that knows no existence at all,
In words that haven't been known or found,
In sayings that don't exist around,
In a nature that has no complexion or bound,
In intentions that have no comprehensive form
In thoughts that have known no thinking at large
And in a world, where to care is to
perish your identity away for it all.

Coordinates — 27.9811° N, 86.8286° E

Forevermore

But if I were to leave tomorrow,
Would you still visit me in your devoted thoughts?
Tell me all the things that reached
your lips, but couldn't fall out?
Like a decayed rose my body rots,
But your memories remain engraved in
my conscience without a healing heart.
Whilst, I live here in a lonesome box,
Your un avowed words, seep in unharmed,
resonating through what remains of my last.
And my entrapped soul leaves now safe and sound.

Coordinates - 27.8547° N, 86.7888° E

Preachers preach

The true nature of morality
is tested in times of desperation.
The only thing that can
bring out the best, the worst, in them.
A mirror of their real reflection,
Morality was born to be unveiled
when humans are starved to their peril.
That's when we see the strength of its foundation,
If the mirror can withhold
the test of desperation, it will give a clean reflection.
If not, it will shatter, the glass pieces
piercing through that person and those around,
And then, finally, will the being be known
for the reality of his innate self and not for the
facade he so systematically wore on the face of it all.

Coordinates – 27.7154° N, 85.3123° E

Fourth law

A body who desires to
belong everywhere,
Ends up nowhere...
An eternal verity of life,
seemingly just and fair.
For his conscience
lacks discernment,
to prioritize which
route to bear....
He ends up on a wall
lonesome and rudderless.

Coordinates – 27°57'32" N, 86°49'29" E

Eureka

What is bad or good....
For me, she may be bad,
For her, he may be good,
But for him I may be bad.
A mad man once told me....
"They called me mad, I lashed out
and there was their reason"
Reaction to an action
Great saints born to
destroy evil, protect man.
Oh! But evil? What is that but
a creation to justify "greater good".
So, when they ask me what is good or bad,
I tell them the mad man's tale and ask them,
What is good or bad?

Coordinates — 27.3938° N, 86.0601° E

Ramechhap Mornings

The wait for the uncertain to become certain... Hope,
anxiousness, fear as the dark gloomy clouds unfold.
The golden ray of hope caged by
the bleak electrifying thunderbolts,
Oh lord save us from the unknown.
It's 7, as I sit to pray, with every second
overwhelming me with dismay.
The pale white faces around me mirror my
'so called' mental state.
I smile at them, and they smile back at me,
As we realize we are on the same page.
The clock strikes 9, the last drop of rain subsides,
Hope, relief and a tint of joy sparkles in our eyes.
The long-lasting wait made us happier than ever,
and that's when I was certain that uncertainty had
become my friend forever.

Coordinates – 27.8069° N, 86.7140° E

Chai-Biscuit Moments

As I sat on the empty lush green grass at Namche,
What caught my eye was the still and
serene mountains that looked my way.
Its calm demeanour intoxicated my whole existence,
I felt a current of optimism energizing me.
Its divine presence teared up my eyes.
Looking up I thanked the lord of ice,
for gifting me this moment to reminisce.

Coordinates – 28.0023° N, 86.8529° E

Everest Base Camp

EBC is the short form for "EVEREST BASE CAMP," located in Nepal. It is a commercial trek for all those who ever wanted to view or be slightly closer to Mt. Everest. For years, trekking enthusiasts have been speaking about this trek. A 14-day expedition and an experience like never before, EBC is ideal for anyone who loves the mountains and wants a realistic experience of what it is to actually climb one.

It is one of my addictive traits to go every summer for a high-altitude trek. A habit I have followed like a tradition since 2018, when I'd done my first trek in Uttarakhand at 16,000ft. Post my graduation, in the summer of 2024, staying loyal to this ritual, I decided to go for EBC—a decision that completely changed how I viewed life and the problems in it.

A large number of trekkers from different countries come for this trek—some young, some old. I met different people, but one common thing I saw in all of them was a fire, a determination to reach the top.

Ramechhap, a small village in Nepal, is where our journey began. The adventure for my team, at least,

Coordinates – 27.9595° N, 86.7899° E

started from here itself. Being a small mountain airport, things are pretty uncertain there. A cloudy weather followed by rains, made it difficult for any flight to take off, and here we were, stranded in this small village for a day with other trekkers like us. With nothing to do, we had only one thing we could do—hope for clear weather. (Not going to mention which one, but one of my thoughts was written here when this incident took place.)

Lukla is the world's highest and most dangerous airport. When we landed there, it was drizzly, but we could immediately feel the smell of the mountains hitting us. Here is where the actual trek began.

There were six camps till EBC (I have given a map of EBC right after this so that anyone reading this can understand what I'm saying and get inspired to go there too). I remember not feeling very up for it at Phakding, my first campsite. That's where I met a trekker from Kazakhstan. A delightful evening—hearing her speak and spending the evening in the backyard facing horses and the mountains—made my sickness feel negligible in front of the vastness of this beauty.

Every day was a challenge of its own. I had four guys in my team; each of them had a personality of their own. We were all from different parts of India, leading completely different lives. In a life away from the mountains, I don't think any of us would ever cross paths, but here the mountains got five uniquely minded individuals together. That's what I mean when I say the mountain has its own magic, and nothing can change that for me.

Usually, during treks, you pitch tents, but since we were staying in offbeat mountain villages, there were lodges called "Nepali teahouses," where trekkers spend the night. Teahouses are cute and warm. The interiors are very earthy, and they have a thriving business of their own because it's the income of the villagers there who depend on this seasonal influx of trekkers.

Trekking, I've learned, is a give and take. You take values, memories, and lessons from the mountains, and what you give in return is homage to its people and respect for it by not littering. To litter on a mountain is a sin; it's like you are disrespecting the person who is feeding you and letting you stay at her home.

When I used to trek, I had this habit of running up, so my guide, a Nepali local called Tul, along with my teammates, started calling me "the mountain girl." There was this one time I reached with the porters—I guess it was in Tengboche, which is the village of a Nepali monastery.

Porters are the backbone of any trek worth its salt. Without them, this system cannot function. They are like superhumans; they carry five to six bags on their backs and walk up like it is nothing much for them. They breathe at ease as if they were at sea level. The way they walk is like a dance—you think it's easy, but then you see the load that they carry and just wonder how they do that.

My porter was, again, a Nepali boy of 20. His name was Navin. The guy used to smoke almost 30 cigarettes a day like a gangster. I remember him lighting up a cigarette at the Everest Base Camp whilst I looked at him in awe. It was like the altitude of 18,000 ft didn't really bother him. I'm pretty sure he must have been like- "Ahh yet another day at the base camp for me. Can we go already? If y'all are done sobbing over this place."

More than reaching a campsite, it is the walk up to there that sticks with you the most. You bond with everyone like never before because each of y'all pushes the other to keep moving. We were no different. Each of us had our days where the rest of us motivated him or her to keep going. Although we didn't trek in a group most of the time, because we were all in our own zones trying to absorb and comprehend the moments in our own way, there were yet times where two to three of us ended up at the same place, and then we used to have long conversations that used to go on for hours.

I still remember gossiping, and since I was the youngest, my trek mates, who were more experienced in life, used to throw in their insightful advice that really stays with me to date. The thing is that the conversations one has on a mountain, will always stay with you. Ask any trekker worth their salt; they will remember the conversations they had with their teammates.

The nights in teahouses used to be spent singing and dancing. I still have videos of me singing with a few people. There was this guy I met who had carried his guitar along with him. He said his dream was to travel and climb with his guitar. He wanted to summit EBC with it.

Another lady, who was 60, was from Canada. She decided to travel from a different side of the globe alone to explore a life she had never lived until then. When one hears such stories, it is very normal to get inspired in a way a city could never inspire you or in a way no other institution could teach you.

It's the best teacher, the best mentor, and your best friend. When life gets lonely, too hard to handle, or if one feels lost, my advice to anyone reading this book is to pack their bags and go for a trek. You will find answers like you never expected. The solace, clarity, and motivation it will give you cannot be found anywhere else.

I can go on and on about this topic since the stories I have etched in my memories cannot be written in two pages. But as they say, some memories are meant to be self-relished because that's the magic in it.

Till date, when my friends and family ask me what I did on that trek, the only thing I tell them in return is, "Words are not enough to describe what I felt and saw."

This was a small insight into a few moments of my 22 days spent in Nepal. I have written this as a call-out to everyone to start trekking or visit the mountains. I was lucky and grateful to witness this magic, and I pray and hope someone takes this as a sign to awaken the explorer within them.

As I once wrote to a friend of mine (inspired by a quote I read), I say this to y'all too:

"The mountains are calling you, and it's time to go."

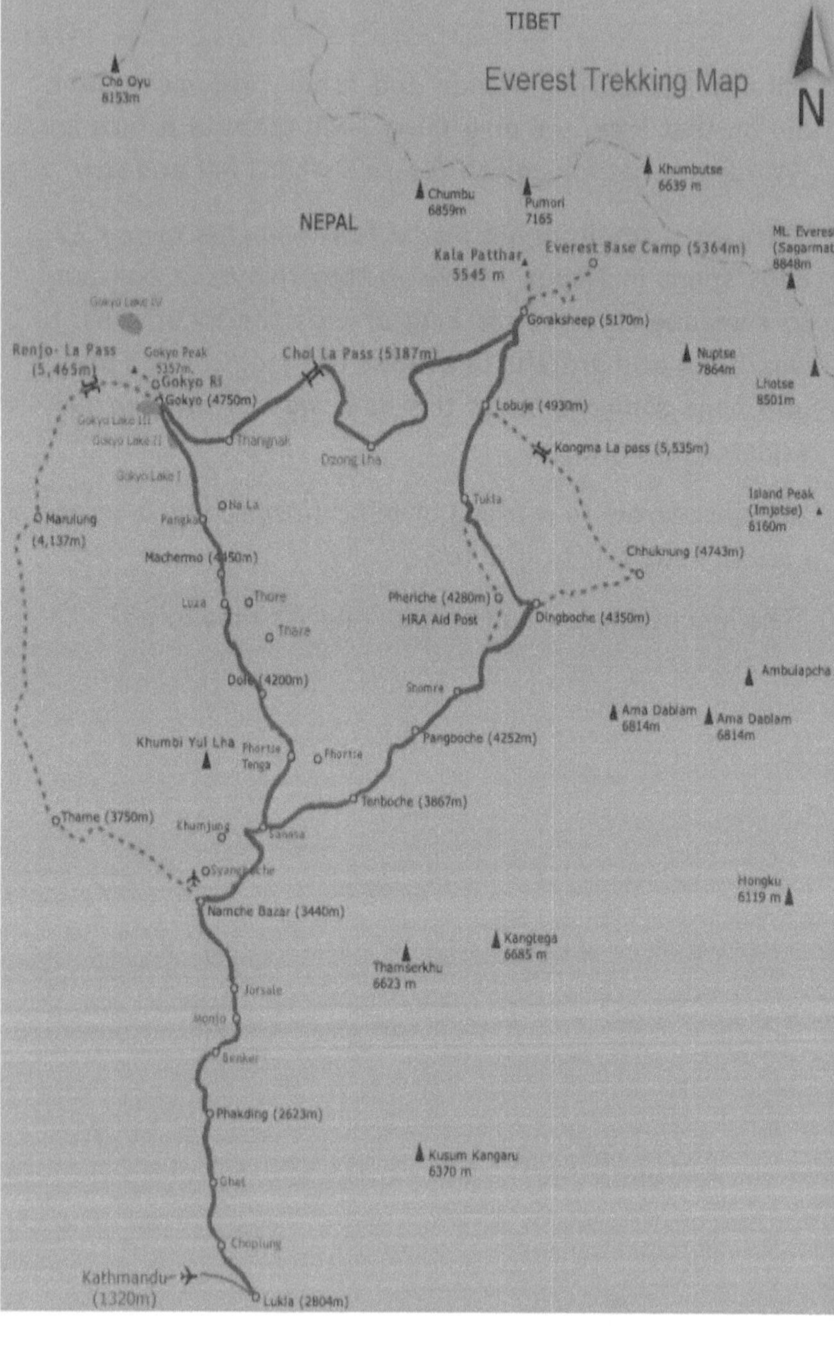

TIBET
Everest Trekking Map
N
Cho Oyu 8153m
Khumbutse 6639 m
Chumbu 6859m
Pumori 7165
NEPAL
Mt. Everest (Sagarmatha) 8848m
Kala Patthar 5545 m
Everest Base Camp (5364m)
Goraksheep (5170m)
Gokyo Lake IV
Renjo La Pass (5,465m)
Gokyo Peak 5357m.
Gokyo Ri
Gokyo (4750m)
Chol La Pass (5387m)
Nuptse 7864m
Lhotse 8501m
Lobuje (4930m)
Kongma La pass (5,535m)
Gokyo Lake III
Gokyo Lake II
Thangnak
Dzong Lha
Gokyo Lake I
Island Peak (Imjatse) 6160m
Marulung (4,137m)
Na La
Tukla
Chhuknung (4743m)
Pangka
Machermo (4450m)
Thore
Pheriche (4280m)
HRA Aid Post
Dingboche (4350m)
Luza
Thare
Ambulapcha
Dole (4200m)
Shomre
Ama Dablam 6814m
Ama Dablam 6814m
Khumbi Yul Lha
Phortse Tenga
Phortse
Pangboche (4252m)
Thame (3750m)
Khumjung
Sanasa
Tenboche (3867m)
Hongku 6119 m
Syangboche
Namche Bazar (3440m)
Kangtega 6685 m
Thamserkhu 6623 m
Jorsale
Monjo
Benkar
Phakding (2623m)
Kusum Kangaru 6370 m
Ghat
Choplung
Kathmandu (1320m)
Lukla (2804m)

The EBC Map

Coordinates — 28.0023° N, 86.8529° E

Trekkers guide

If any of y'all reading this come to this page and think about packing your bags to wander off into the mountains for a trek or just a hike, this page is for those new born adventure junkies.

When I was 15 and did my first high-altitude trek — Roopkund (Uttarakhand) — my elder sister, who is an experienced mountaineer, gave me some advice. A few of these lessons I learned while trekking alone, and I would like to share them with anyone who reads these pages and feels the slightest pull to hear their calling and take that life-changing leap of faith in themselves and the process of the mountains.

Here are a few things to keep in mind as someone going on their first trek:

- **Go prepared physically for a high-altitude trek.** By training physically, I don't mean just going to the gym. Engage in high-intensity cardio and exercises to strengthen your calves, glutes, and lungs.

- **Incorporate running and climbing.** Running for 30 minutes every day, climbing 25 floors with a 10 kg bag and weights on your ankles, swimming,

Coordinates — 27.8923° N, 86.8314° E

and doing light-weighted workouts are a must to follow.

- **Trekking is a mental game.** Although it's physically demanding, trekking ultimately comes down to willpower. There will be times you may feel like you can't go on, but the euphoric feeling you get when reaching the top is what will keep you going.

- **Take it one step at a time.** All that matters is the step in front of you. The rest can be thought about after taking that step.

- **Focus on breathing and staying calm.** The rest will follow through. Do not try to rush — it's not a race. The old saying, "Slow and steady wins the race," comes in handy on a mountain.

- **Enjoy the journey.** Don't get so focused on reaching the top that you forget to enjoy the journey. Most of your trek is the journey itself, and that's where you'll learn the most valuable lessons. (This is something I learned on one of my treks.)

- **Be open to learning.** Take the best from your fellow teammates and be open to new views on life.

- **Adjust and work as a team.** True trekkers know the value of teamwork and leading by example. Always be the last one to leave from a difficult situation.

- **Prepare for unpredictable weather.** Weather on a mountain is the most unpredictable factor. One moment you may experience 40-degree sunlight, and the next, a hailstorm. Being prepared for these uncertainties makes you resourceful.

- **Carry extra supplies.** Always carry extra pairs of everything you're bringing because, up there, you won't have any other option.

- **Learn how to use a sleeping bag.** Buy a sleeping bag and liner and practice getting in and out of it. This is a skill no one will mention, but everyone struggles with.

- **Respect the environment.** Do not waste food or litter on the mountain. Carry disposable bags at all times, and once you reach the base camp, dispose them off properly.

- **Don't worry about lagging behind.** Lagging behind doesn't make you weak. No one is there to judge you because the fact that you're up there makes you a go-getter.

- **Research about your trek.** Always read and learn about the trek and the terrain you'll be walking and climbing on. This preparation will keep you ready in advance.

- **Hydrate and eat well.** THIS!!! My friends is the most important thing, again coming from my personal experience. Drink water every

30 minutes. Hydrate and eat very well because, trust me, that is your fuel. You may feel like you're not hungry or thirsty, but it's what you need the most — it's your bank balance on a mountain.

- **Carry a diary.** Your mind will have stories you'll want to write down.

- **Enjoy and loosen up.** Have some fun because these are the days and moments you live for. ☺

PACK IT IN
PACK IT OUT
BY PARKS PROJECT®
IN PARTNERSHIP WITH LEAVE NO TRACE™

Pack it in, Pack it out

Do It the Right Way – Carry an Eco Bag!
We call it the "Pack It In, Pack It Out" method. An eco bag, similar to a fanny pack, can be worn around your waist while trekking. During hikes, we often come across litter carelessly left behind on trails. Instead of ignoring it, the right thing to do is pick up any waste you encounter to help preserve the mountain's natural beauty and biodiversity.
Waste management is everyone's responsibility—not just the waste we produce ourselves but also what others leave behind. By cleaning up, we give back to nature and protect the environment for future trekkers. Pack out your waste responsibly! Carry it down to base camp and dispose it off properly in designated bins. Remember, even biodegradable waste takes time to decompose in mountain environments.
For years, the trekking community has been advocating for green trekking and responsible tourism to promote a cleaner, greener environment.
Let's all do our part!

How we leave mountains better than we found them:

Our Green Trails vision is to leave mountain trails better than we find them. To do this, we deep dive into our trek practices and protocols to see how we can make ourselves carbon negative. These are our **GOLDEN 6** practices. These practices also help increase the carrying capacity of the mountains, helping more people to experience the goodness of the mountains at minimal environmental cost.

When any of us plan for a trek, we plan for gear, we plan for the route, we plan for safety to a certain extent. We hardly plan for how to trek in a way that causes the least impact. This is not a common thought. Sustainability has become an afterthought and that is a shame. We need to change that. We need to look at everything we do, everything we bring to the trek and see how to be efficient and least damaging to the environment. That is the challenge of the Green Trails. We are relentlessly working to rethink trekking and bring in innovations and practices that will simplify trekking. We want to trek in a way where we give back to the mountains. When we crack this, we will have a reality where everyone can trek and trek sustainably.

G1 How Green Sweep has left our Mountains Visibly Cleaner

Our trekkers and our team with the help of our Eco bags clean the waste off our trails. We clean around 20,000 kgs of harmful litter (plastic, glass, metal, etc.) every year.

G2 No Waste is Waste If it Is Segregated

Every piece of waste collected is segregated. Every segregated waste is a waste that does not have to enter a landfill. Since 2016, we consistently divert more than 50% waste from reaching landfills.

G3 How Composting Turns Kitchen Waste To Manure:

We manage all kitchen waste at source by composting it. In 2 months, it turns into fertile manure. 100% of our kitchen waste is composted at source, thereby not adding to greenhouse gas emissions.

G4 How Our Bio Toilets Give Back To The Environment

At Indiahikes, we use specially designed Bio Toilets capable of composting human waste in mountain environments. Till now our Bio Toilets will convert over 20,000 kgs of human waste into rich compost for the mountains every year.

G5 How Redesigning Washing Systems Reduces Water Footprint

Water is a scarce resource in the mountains. So we go to great lengths to reduce the water we consume on our trek. Our washing systems have helped us reduce

G6 Be more Energy Efficient

Be it solar panels for powering our campsite lights to redesigning our gas stoves in the kitchen, we work on ensuring efficient energy consumption on our treks.

Leave No Trace

the art of leaving mountains better than we found them...

- ➢ **Plan & Prepare Ahead** - Understand the regulations, terrain, and potential hazards of your trekking route. This helps you avoid bad weather, emergencies, and unnecessary risks. Trek in small groups and always carry a map and compass instead of marking or flagging trails.

- ➢ **Segregate Waste** - Proper waste segregation reduces landfill waste and helps protect the environment. Every bit sorted makes a difference!

- ➢ **Leave Nature Untouched** - Preserve the landscape by leaving rocks, flowers, and natural artifacts undisturbed. Avoid digging trenches or altering the terrain.

- ➢ **Minimize Campfire Impact** - Use lightweight stoves for cooking and candle lanterns for lighting. If making a fire: Keep it small and use dry sticks found on the ground. Burn wood completely to ash, extinguish fires fully, and cool the ashes. Dig a 4-5 inch fire pit to minimize impact. Travel & Camp on Durable Surfaces- Stick to established trails, campsites, dry grass, or snow to prevent erosion. Camp at least 200m from water sources to protect riparian areas. Good campsites are found, not made— avoid disturbing untouched areas.

- ➢ **The Green Sweep** - Follow the Pack It In, Pack It Out method— carry out all waste and leave no trace.

- ➢ **Respect Locals & Wildlife** - Keep noise levels low—loud music disturbs wildlife and fellow trekkers. Secure waste properly to prevent animals from accessing it.

- ➢ **Be courteous to locals** - Respect their space, greet them kindly, and avoid disrupting their daily routines.

- ➢ **Reduce Your Water Footprint** - Purify water from streams and rivers using filters or treatment tablets instead of relying on bottled water. Follow local guidelines to avoid contaminating natural water sources.

Trekkers Checklist

Essential Gear
□ Backpack (40-60L) - Comfortable & well-fitted
□ Daypack (10-20L) - For short hikes & summit day
□ Trekking Poles - Adjustable & lightweight
Clothing (Layering is Key!)
□ Base Layer (Moisture-Wicking) - Thermal top & bottom
□ Insulation Layer - Fleece/down jacket
□ Outer Layer (Waterproof & Windproof) - Jacket & pants
□ Trekking Pants - Quick-dry & breathable
□ Full-Sleeve Shirts - UV protection & warmth
□ Gloves - Inner thermal + waterproof outer gloves
□ Hat/Cap - Sun protection & woolen cap for cold
□ Neck Gaiter/Balaclava - Protects from wind & dust
□ Socks (3-4 pairs) - Woolen + moisture-wicking socks
□ Gaiters - To keep snow & debris out of shoes
Footwear
□ High-Ankle Trekking Boots - Waterproof & well-broken-in
□ Camp Shoes/Sandals - For relaxation at campsites
Sleeping Gear
□ Sleeping Bag (-10°C to -20°C rated) - Depending on altitude
□ Sleeping Mat - Insulation & comfort
Navigation & Safety
□ Map & Compass/GPS Device - Essential for navigation
□ Headlamp + Extra Batteries - For night treks & camps
□ Whistle & Multi-Tool/Knife - Emergency use
□ First Aid Kit - Painkillers, bandages, antiseptic, altitude sickness meds
□ Personal Medications - Any prescribed medicines
□ Sunscreen (SPF 50+) - High-altitude UV protection
□ Lip Balm (SPF-rated) - Prevents chapping
□ Sunglasses (UV-Protected, Category 3 or 4) - Protects against snow blindness
Hydration & Nutrition
□ Water Bottles (2-3L capacity) - Hydration is crucial
□ Water Purification (Tablets/Filter/UV Steripen) - Safe drinking water
□ Electrolyte Sachets - Prevent dehydration
□ High-Energy Snacks - Nuts, protein bars, dry fruits, chocolates
Miscellaneous & Extras
□ Trekking Permits & ID - Required for entry
□ Emergency Contact Info - Keep it handy
□ Towel & Wet Wipes - Biodegradable preferred
□ Toiletries (Biodegradable Soap & Toothpaste) - Leave no trace
□ Toilet Paper & Ziplock Bags - For waste disposal
□ Hand Sanitizer & Face Mask - Hygiene essentials
□ Camera/GoPro & Power Bank - Capture the adventure!
Optional but Useful
□ Microspikes/Crampons - If trekking on snow/ice
□ Oximeter - Monitor oxygen levels
□ Notebook & Pen - Journaling the experience
□ Lightweight Book/Kindle - For downtime

EMERGENCY SURVIVAL CHECKLIST

TOOLKIT
NECKWARMER
WHISTLE
FIRST AID KIT
OXYMETER
EXTRA WATER
MATCHSTICKS OR LIGHTERS

torchlight
portable heater
compass
sun/snow glasses
canned food items
camping stove burner
walkie talkie
extra gloves

The Math of Backpacking

Packing your backpack

With a backpack, organization and easy access are key. Use these essential packing tips as a guide.

Store essentials such as sunscreen, a compass, maps, and guidebooks in an outer pocket

Waterproof bags should be used to store items that must stay dry, particularly spare clothing and your sleeping bag

Carry your water bottle upright where it's accessible

Lighter items such as sleeping mats and bags should remain at the bottom of the backpack

Coordinates — 27.7154° N, 85.3123° E

Acknowledgement

I would like to dedicate this page to all those extraordinary individuals without whom I wouldn't have been able to reach here and write this very book.

Firstly, my mother, **Sonali Parikh**-I owe everything to her. My very own strong wonder woman who inspires me to outperform myself every day. Spending time with her clears my thoughts and grounds me as an individual.

My father, **Major Anuj Parikh (retd)**, mentored me, gave me the very idea of writing this book, and taught me that it is never too late to achieve your utmost potential. He has been a constant support in all my endeavors.

Radhika Parikh, my elder sister, is the very reason I started trekking. I owe everything I've learned about the mountains to her. An experienced mountaineer and rock climber with so many feathers in her cap, she continues to be the ideal trailblazer for me. I also want to thank her for writing such a lovely foreword.

My dear grandparents (Mamama and Ajja)—their warmth and moral support mean the world to me.

I am very grateful to the respected and renowned writer, **Mr. Kamlesh Tripathi**, for his advice and guidance while writing this book.

To my workplace, **Ma-th (Marching Ants and Trigger Happy)**, for opening up the creative chambers of my mind and helping me hone my skills as a writer.

Some of my thoughts were inspired by the sayings of **my fellow teammates and my trek guide- Tul**. I thank them for enriching my experience on the mountains.

My direct connection to these thoughts are linked with the people I met during my treks—the locals, the porters—some names I don't remember anymore, but the feelings they left behind inspired me to write down these thoughts.

A special shoutout to my dear, talented friend - **Hardika Lad**, for designing and painting my cover page, which turned out just the way I had imagined.

Finally, I thank my dear readers for reaching the end of this book and being patient throughout the read. This wouldn't be a complete journey without you all.

Author's Letter

Dear Readers,

If I've managed to ignite your love for trekking and backpacking, and you've gone through all my guidelines but still feel confused or have questions about something I may not have covered, don't hesitate to reach out.

If there's a particular thought that resonated with you and you'd like to know more about it, feel free to ask. I'd be more than happy to answer your questions!

See yaa....until next time.

Lots of Love,

Srish

Instagram – @srishti_pai

Business email – paisrisht@gmail.com

The end